MW01708697

Media
Literacy Response Forms

Grades 4-6

Written by Marie-Helen Goyetche
& Eleanor M. Summers
Illustrated by S&S Learning Materials

About the authors:
Marie-Helen Goyetche is an elementary school teacher and a freelance writer. She has published over 100 articles and over 30 curriculum books.

Eleanor Summers is a retired elementary teacher who continues to be involved in education– in and out of school. This is her seventh teacher resource book in language arts.

ISBN: 978-1-55035-893-3

Published in the U.S.A by:
On The Mark Press
3909 Witmer Road PMB 175
Niagara Falls, New York
14305
www.onthemarkpress.com

Published in Canada by:
S&S Learning Materials
15 Dairy Avenue
Napanee, Ontario
K7R 1M4
www.sslearning.com

 "We acknowledge the financial support of the Government of Canada through the Book Publishing Industry Development Program (BPIDP) for this project."

At A Glance

Learning Expectations	Identifying Information	Characters	Summarizing	Critical Thinking	Vocabulary	Creativity
Understanding Concepts						
Identifying parts of speech – nouns, verbs, adjectives					•	
Identifying literary devices such as: similes, metaphors, synonyms, prefixes, suffixes, root words, atmosphere	•	•		•	•	•
Use connecting words (first, then, next) to retell a story			•			
Use a dictionary and thesaurus to expand vocabulary					•	
Reading Comprehension						
Make predictions based on evidence from the text				•		
Identify and describe story elements	•		•	•	•	
Identify main idea, provide supporting details, key words	•		•	•	•	•
Summarize story elements, cite supporting evidence	•		•	•		
Explain how story elements relate to each other		•				
Retell the story by adapting it for presentation in another way			•			
Identify and describe character traits, and cite supporting evidence		•		•		•
Identify and describe similarities and differences		•				•
Identify cause and effect relationships	•					
Make connections between the story and personal experiences/the real world	•			•		
Make inferences based on personal interpretation of the media	•	•		•		
Make judgments and draw conclusions using evidence from the media	•	•				•
Create a media text or advertisement	•	•		•		•
Creative writing – sequel to the story, join the story, rewrite the ending	•	•	•	•		•
Forms of writing – book reviews, book report, biography, letter to a character		•		•		•
Express own interpretation of a story through visual and performing arts (illustrations, picture book, theatrical script, book cover)						•
Develop opinions and express personal points of view		•				
Identify the point of view of the author or a character		•				
Distinguish between fact and fiction or true or false using evidence from text			•	•	•	

Table of Contents

Teacher Assessment Rubric

Student's Name: ______________________________

Put a check mark ✓ in the box that indicates the student's level of achievement.

Level 1: requires assistance; inconsistent effort; shows limited understanding of concepts
Level 2: requires minimal assistance; shows limited understanding of concepts
Level 3: independent; consistent effort; shows general understanding of concepts
Level 4: independent; consistent effort; shows thorough understanding of concepts

Criteria	Level 1	Level 2	Level 3	Level 4
Vocabulary Development				
• Understands the text at word level				
• Recognizes and understands media specific language				
Identifying Important Information				
• Identifies the message and main idea of media				
• Evaluates story elements and conclusions				
• Draws conclusions based on personal interpretation				
Character Analysis				
• Demonstrates an understanding of character traits				
• Uses knowledge of character roles to evaluate roles and gives supporting details from media				
Summarizing Events				
• Retells story in proper sequence with supporting details				
• Identifies and describes story elements				
Reasoning and Critical Thinking				
• Makes connection between media form and real world				
• Makes judgments and draws conclusions using evidence from the story				
• Uses evidence to make predictions and inferences				
• Develops opinions and expresses personal point of view				
Creativity and Design				
• Create a media text: advertisement, poster				
• Create a non-text media: commercial, talk show interview, radio broadcast				
• Express own interpretation through visual and performing arts				

Student Self-Assessment Rubric

Name: ______________________________ **Date:** ______________

Put a check mark ✓ in the box that best describes your performance.
Then add your points to determine your total score.

Expectations	My Performance				
	Always (4 points)	Frequently (3 points)	Sometimes (2 points)	Needs Improvement (1 point)	My Points
✓ I remained focused and on task.					
✓ I asked for explanations and assistance when needed.					
✓ I was prepared and organized.					
✓ I used my text to support ideas.					
✓ I used my own experiences and knowledge to support my predictions.					
✓ I used all available resources.					
✓ I rechecked the information so I could rethink my answers.					
✓ I edited and proofread my work.					
✓ I know what I am good at.					
✓ I know what I need to work on.					

Total Points: __________

The most valuable thing I learned was: ______________________________

____

Media Response Forms

Planning and Implementation Guide

Why Use Media Response Forms?

- Media awareness is the process by which the learner derives meaning from media and from his or her prior knowledge. It involves thinking before, during, and after the media experience. Assessment of media awareness and comprehension can only be done indirectly because it is a thought process.
- Media response forms help you to assess your students' understanding of the media they are encountering. The activities in this resource encourage students to make creative connections between media and their previous learning. This connection strengthens their awareness and comprehension.
- Media response forms are inviting, meaningful activities that students can complete independently during a Language Arts program. This provides classroom time for you to conduct small group instruction and assistance, or to conference with individual students.
- These worksheets provide accurate assessment information on student skill levels. An analysis of completed activities will assist you in determining the next steps in your planning and programming to meet individual student needs.

NOTE: While media is a huge part of modern life, be aware that not all students will have equal access to all media. Computers, television, newspapers, and magazines play varying roles in today's homes. Be cautious and either give students choice to avoid media they personally do not have access to, or ensure they have access to it during class time.

Introducing Media Response Forms in a Mini-Lesson:

- Media response forms should be introduced to the whole class after a discussion or a mini-lesson. Select a media that supports the skill focus of the worksheet you are introducing.
- Step by step, teach your students the skill focus of the response form by using an enlarged copy of the worksheets on an overhead, chart paper, or chalkboard. Explain the concepts being introduced using the "think aloud" strategy to model your thinking as you complete the form. Students can see and understand the process you go through to respond. Involve the students in a guided practice by asking them questions, encouraging discussion, and recording a variety of their responses. Be sure to highlight the range of possibilities of appropriate responses.
- After the mini-lesson, have the students practice completing the worksheet as a response to a chosen type of media.
- Use this mini-lesson format to introduce each new media response form.
- Once several response forms have been taught and modeled, and the students have had sufficient practice, the worksheets can be used as an independent response activity for shared, guided, or independent comprehension assessment.

- Introduce media response forms based on the individual and collective learning needs of your students. You may wish to introduce worksheets from all six skill areas so that students can develop a range of skills at varying levels of difficulty.

Organizing Media Response Forms:

- Media response forms can be organized in a variety of ways. Students can be given a package/folder of media response forms to complete within a specified time frame during Language Arts class. You may also wish to designate the number of worksheets that must be completed.

- Alternatively, the worksheets may be kept in labeled folders or bins, and students may be given a free choice to select the response form that best suits their chosen media. Ensure that students are aware of how many forms they must complete and how much time they have to complete the tasks.

- The response forms can also be used to show a similar response to different media. For example, write a biography on a character from a commercial, TV show, magazine or Internet article.

- Alternate the response forms that are available so that they can develop, master, and practice a variety of skills. Providing variety will help to ensure that student motivation remains strong.

Sharing Responses:

- Allow time for students to share their responses so that they may celebrate their accomplishments. Sharing helps to develop motivated learners who acquire new ideas from peers and recommend media materials to each other. Sharing also helps to foster self-confidence in individual students as they present and discuss their responses.

- Sharing can be done weekly, as a whole class, or through individual assignments. Presentations can be to the whole class or to small groups. Displaying student work on bulletin boards increases sharing of ideas.

Helping Students Select Appropriate Media Formats:

- Try to determine the level of skill your students have with specific media.

  1. Do they know the parts of a magazine and how to choose an article?
  2. Do they know how to use the Internet to find an article?
  3. Do they have experience with reading a newspaper and know how to find specific articles of interest to them?
  4. Do they know how to view TV shows and movies for purposes other than entertainment? Do they know how to view critically?
  5. Do they understand media and the message and power they have?

You may have to review, or even teach, some of these skills before beginning to work on completing response forms. It makes sense to begin with forms where students have the most experience and comfort.

Tracking, Assessment, and Individual Programming:

- The Personal Media Response Record (p. 14) and Media Response Tracking Sheet (p. 15) are to be completed by each student independently. These are useful tools for monitoring independent response activity and skill area completion.

- A collection of the student's completed media response forms provides an extensive overview of his/her media comprehension skills. Student-Teacher Conferences may be conducted to gather performance-based assessment information and direct individual programming. Consider the format on the conference form provided (p. 12) to bring structure to your conferences.

- The assessment rubrics (p. 4 and 5) are useful aids for gathering information on a student's strengths and needs. These rubrics should be used to direct independent instruction and mini-lessons. They will also provide feedback to students on their progress and guide them in setting personal learning goals.

Modeling the Media Response Form Activities

Students may complete these forms during, or after, reading or viewing. They may expand upon their answers by providing supporting evidence on the back of the worksheet.

In this section you will find suggestions for modeling the six different types of response forms in your mini-lessons. The first one, using the Common and Proper Nouns worksheet as an example of a Vocabulary Development activity, is described in detail from start to finish of the mini-lesson. You may adapt this modeling format to introduce any of the media response forms in this resource. Be sure to read **Introducing Media Response Forms in a Mini-Lesson (p. 6-7)** prior to reading the modeling suggestions below.

Vocabulary Development:

These worksheets focus on the analysis of language conventions used in the media materials and a development of understanding of language terms that are specific to media. As students build their understanding of vocabulary and language structures, they develop a deeper understanding of the media message.

Example: Common and Proper Nouns (p. 16)

- At the start of the mini-lesson, give (or review) the definition of a common noun (a person, animal, place, or thing) and a proper noun (a specific person, animal, place or thing – the noun begins with a capital letter)

- While reading (magazine or Internet article), ask the student to watch and listen for common and proper nouns in the text.

- Midway through the section, stop reading and have the students do a Think-Pair-Share activity. Record a few of the students' responses on the chalkboard/chart before continuing. Write their answers under the headings "Common Nouns" and "Proper Nouns". Repeat the same procedure once you have finished reading the section.

- Then, using the response form template, ask the students to identify a sentence from the material that they would like to examine. Write the sentence on the chalkboard and have the students identify the common and proper nouns. Ask them to then explain why they think this word is a common or a proper noun. By explaining their reasoning, the exercise becomes more meaningful, and they are more likely to remember what is a common noun and what is a proper noun. Repeat this process to complete the form.

Identifying Important Information:

In this section, students learn to distinguish between important and extraneous information, and identify main ideas. Students will also learn about specific language structures used in their texts, such as metaphors and similes.

Example: Analyzing the Message (p. 30)

- Begin the mini-lesson by telling the students that they will be learning to identify important information in the story, and reflecting on what it means to each of them by relating it to their personal experiences.
- Ask the students to look for literary devices. Remind students what literary devices are and have them find many different kinds or have the students focus on one or two.
- Once the students have identified a literary device example, have them record their answers under the heading "What was said?". Ask them to explain it in their own words (in everyday English).
- Have them exchange their findings in small groups and correct it if the student did find a literary device. Through group discussion, analyze how the student gave a correct and easy explanation.

Character Analysis:

These worksheets focus the students' attention on the characters in TV shows, film, movies and people written about in articles found in newspapers, magazines, or the Internet. Who are these characters? How do they live? How do they solve their problems? Readers are challenged to identify similarities and differences between themselves and the characters, and between the characters and people they know. Characters are frequently the most memorable part of visual and written media for children. Analyzing the behaviors of these characters helps bring them to life, and engages students in such thought provoking questions as "What would this character be like if he or she lived in my city, or even next door?" and "If you were to become this character, what would you do different or similar?"

Example: Personality Web (p. 38)

- Start the mini-lesson by telling the students that they will be analyzing a text to identify character traits of the main character. Define character traits as the way a character behaves, looks, thinks, feels, and responds to others in the story.
- Introduce the TV show, film, or movie and identify the main character that you will be analyzing. Ask the students to think about his or her character traits as you watch this character in action.

- Begin watching, and pause it midway through to check for understanding. Have the students do a Think-Pair-Share activity, focusing on the traits they have heard about so far. Record a few responses on the form before continuing the show.

Summarizing Events:

These worksheets focus on reviewing the elements of a material. Story elements include the setting, characters, problem, events, and the solution/resolution of the story. The 5 W's (Who, What, Where, When, Why) are often used together with How to prompt the retelling of a story. Readers are challenged to retell the story in the sequence it occurred. Each story element is a crucial component to the story, so every element must be remembered during the retell on the response activity.

Example: Story Trail (p. 50)

- Tell the students they will be learning how to retell a story using story elements. Define story elements as the setting, characters, problems, events, and solution/resolution of the story.
- Introduce the article (newspaper, magazine, Internet) and identify the subject to be summarized. Remind the students to focus on identifying the story elements as you read.
- Begin reading, and stop midway through the section to check for understanding. Have the students do a Think-Pair-Share activity, focusing on story elements they have described so far. Record a few responses on the form before continuing the reading.
- Repeat the same procedure once you have finished reading the section. Record a few of the students' examples for the remaining boxes on the form. Ask them to confirm whether or not their responses are story elements based on the definition you provided.

Reasoning and Critical Thinking:

These exercises require students to evaluate and modify the text using their own ideas, experiences, and imagination. Readers are challenged to bring new life to the story by adding new characters, joining the story, and changing the ending, etc. By applying their knowledge of the story in these ways, they have opportunities to develop an advanced level of comprehension and demonstrate higher-order thinking skills.

Example: Believe It or Not (p. 66)

- Start the mini-lesson by telling the students that, as a group, they will be learning about useful and safe practices on the Internet. They will use their findings to create a Do's and Don'ts list for younger students.
- Introduce web sites such as Yahoo, MSN, and Google and the articles found through them. Tell the students to be critical of what they are seeing and to look at it as if they were younger.
- In pairs, the students can discuss and write down tips as they come across the information read on the Internet.

- Repeat the same procedure for the student to have at least four tips on what to do and what not to do. As a whole class activity, put all the answers on the book to collectively create a listing of Do's and Don'ts.

Creativity and Design:

These exercises require students to think outside the box using their own ideas, experiences, and imagination. Readers are challenged to bring new life to the story by adding new characters, joining the story, and changing the ending, etc. By applying their knowledge of the story in these ways, they have opportunities to develop an advanced level of comprehension and demonstrate higher-order thinking skills.

Example: Picture Book Design (p. 80)

- Start the mini-lesson by telling the students that they will individually choose an article or short movie they have enjoyed.

- They will create a children's picture using the information and/or story line found in the piece they enjoyed.

- They can use the boxes to help lay out the pictures and the important events within the article or story. Have them write the story in simple language.

- In pairs, the students can edit and make suggestions to their partner.

- Once the draft is done, the students then use white $8^{1/2}$ x 11 paper to illustrate and rewrite their story.

- Once their book is complete, have them read their new picture book to younger students.

Teacher – Student Conference Form

Student's name: ______________________________ **Date:** ________________

Title: ______________________________ **Type of Media:** ____________

Record of Student's Retelling:

- Identifies setting, time, and place. **Yes** **No**
- Names main character. **Yes** **No**
- States main character's problem. **Yes** **No**
- Mentions other characters. **Yes** **No**
- Uses story vocabulary in the retelling. **Yes** **No**
- Identifies main idea and provides supporting details. **Yes** **No**

Comments: ____

____

____

Provides plot details in sequential order. **Yes** **No**

Comments: ____

____

Makes inferences. **Yes** **No**

Comments: ____

____

Makes connections with the text. **Yes** **No**

Comments: ____

____

Additional Comments: ____

____

Media Literacy Response Forms

List of Work Sheets

Vocabulary Development

1. Common and Proper Nouns
2. This Mail's for You
3. Amazing Adjectives
4. Word Search
5. Lights! Camera! Action!
6. All About Atmosphere
7. A Picture is Worth 1000 Words
8. Calling All Parts of Speech!
9. Media Symbols
10. What's My Line?
11. TV Types
12. Elements of a TV Show

Character Analysis

1. Personality Web
2. Character's Behavior Evidence
3. Addition of a New Character
4. People Behind the Scenes
5. Character Comparison
6. Nonfiction into Fiction
7. True or False
8. My Friend
9. Write a Letter of Advice
10. What would YOU Do?
11. The Ins and Outs of the Character
12. Biography

Reasoning and Critical Thinking

1. My TV Show
2. For Your Information
3. What to Watch
4. Dear Producer
5. Fact or Opinion
6. KWLQ
7. Believe It or Not!
8. Ad Awareness
9. Adding Important Details
10. Emotions

Identifying Important Information

1. Article Reporting
2. What's the Message?
3. Analyzing the Message
4. Who Is Your Target Audience?
5. Problem Solver
6. Behind the Scenes
7. Picture Analysis
8. Changing Consumers
9. Five Senses
10. Cause and Effect Fishbone

Summarizing Events

1. Story Trail
2. It Goes Like This!
3. It's All About Time
4. Comic Strip
5. Bookmark Organizer
6. Nonfiction Report
7. Extra! Extra!
8. Sentence Sum Up
9. The Funnies!
10. Find and Flag!

Creativity and Design

1. Putting the Best Foot Forward
2. Design a Costume
3. Photo Journal
4. Create a TV Schedule
5. And the Survey Says...
6. Switching the Feelings
7. Movie Poster
8. Create a Slogan
9. Jingle Along
10. Changing the Ending
11. Picture Book Design

Media Literacy Response – Personal Record

Name:____'s media response record.

Genre Key: **P** – Print **TV** – Television **M/V** – Movie/Video **I** – Internet

Date	Title	Author	Genre

Media Literacy Response Forms

Tracking Sheet ☑ **Name:** ______________________________

Vocabulary Development

- ❑ 1. Common and Proper Nouns
- ❑ 2. This Mail's for You!
- ❑ 3. Amazing Adjectives
- ❑ 4. Word Search
- ❑ 5. Lights! Camera! Action!
- ❑ 6. All About Atmosphere
- ❑ 7. A Picture is Worth 1000 Words
- ❑ 8. Calling All Parts of Speech!
- ❑ 9. Media Symbols
- ❑ 10. What's My Line?
- ❑ 11. TV Types
- ❑ 12. Elements of a TV Show

Character Analysis

- ❑ 1. Personality Web
- ❑ 2. Character's Behavior Evidence
- ❑ 3. Addition of a New Character
- ❑ 4. People Behind the Scenes
- ❑ 5. Character Comparison
- ❑ 6. Nonfiction into Fiction
- ❑ 7. True or False
- ❑ 8. My Friend
- ❑ 9. Write a Letter of Advice
- ❑ 10. What would YOU Do?
- ❑ 11. The Ins and Outs of the Character
- ❑ 12. Biography

Reasoning and Critical Thinking

- ❑ 1. My TV Show
- ❑ 2. For Your Information
- ❑ 3. What to Watch
- ❑ 4. Dear Producer
- ❑ 5. Fact or Opinion
- ❑ 6. KWLQ
- ❑ 7. Believe It or Not!
- ❑ 8. Ad Awareness
- ❑ 9. Adding Important Details
- ❑ 10. Emotions

Identifying Important Information

- ❑ 1. Article Reporting
- ❑ 2. What's the Message?
- ❑ 3. Analyzing the Message
- ❑ 4. Who Is Your Target Audience?
- ❑ 5. Problem Solver
- ❑ 6. Behind the Scenes
- ❑ 7. Picture Analysis
- ❑ 8. Changing Consumers
- ❑ 9. Five Senses
- ❑ 10. Cause and Effect Fishbone

Summarizing Events

- ❑ 1. Story Trail
- ❑ 2. It Goes Like This!
- ❑ 3. It's All About Time!
- ❑ 4. Comic Strip
- ❑ 5. Bookmark Organizer
- ❑ 6. Nonfiction Report
- ❑ 7. Extra! Extra!
- ❑ 8. Sentence Sum Up
- ❑ 9. The Funnies!
- ❑ 10. Find and Flag!

Creativity and Design

- ❑ 1. Putting the Best Foot Forward
- ❑ 2. Design a Costume
- ❑ 3. Photo Journal
- ❑ 4. Create A TV Schedule
- ❑ 5. And the Survey Says…
- ❑ 6. Switching the Feelings
- ❑ 7. Movie Poster
- ❑ 8. Create A Slogan
- ❑ 9. Jingle Along
- ❑ 10. Changing the Ending
- ❑ 11. Picture Book Design

Vocabulary Development 1

Name: ______________________

Date: ______________________

Media: ______________________

- ▶ Newspaper
- ▶ Magazine
- ▶ Internet Article
- ☐ TV Show
- ☐ Movie
- ☐ Video

Common and Proper Nouns

A **common noun** names a person, animal, place, or thing. A **proper noun** names a specific person, animal, place, or thing. **Proper nouns** begin with a capital.

Read your written media. Find **10 common nouns** and **10 proper nouns** in the article. Write them under the correct heading on the chart.

Common Nouns	Proper Nouns
1.	1.
2.	2.
3.	3.
4.	4.
5.	5.
6.	6.
7.	7.
8.	8.
9.	9.
10.	10.

Vocabulary Development 2

Name: ______________________________

Date: ______________________________

Media: ______________________________

▶ Newspaper ☐ TV Show

▶ Magazine ☐ Movie

▶ Internet Article ☐ Video

This Mail's for You!

Read your article. Select **10 key words** that are important and write them on the lines below.

1. ______________________ **6.** ______________________

2. ______________________ **7.** ______________________

3. ______________________ **8.** ______________________

4. ______________________ **9.** ______________________

5. ______________________ **10.** ______________________

Now write an e-mail to a friend about the article. Use the 10 words in your e-mail.

To: ______________________________

Cc: ______________________________

Subject: ______________________________

Vocabulary Development 3

Name: ______________________

Date: ______________________

Media: ______________________

▶ Newspaper ☐ TV Show
▶ Magazine ☐ Movie
▶ Internet Article ☐ Video

Amazing Adjectives

Adjectives are words that **describe** or tell us about **nouns**.

Read your article. Look for words that tell you about the characters or the setting. Find and write five adjectives from the article that describe the characters and five that describe the setting. Write your own "amazing adjectives" that could be used to describe the characters and setting. Complete the chart.

	Characters	**Setting**
Adjectives from the article		
My own "amazing adjectives"		

Vocabulary Development 4

Name: ______________________________

Date: ______________________________

Media: ______________________________

▶ Newspaper ☐ TV Show

▶ Magazine ☐ Movie

▶ Internet Article ☐ Video

Word Search

Read your article. Select 20 interesting words. Write the words in the Word Box.

1. ____________	6. ____________	11. ____________	16. ____________
2. ____________	7. ____________	12. ____________	17. ____________
3. ____________	8. ____________	13. ____________	18. ____________
4. ____________	9. ____________	14. ____________	19. ____________
5. ____________	10. ____________	15. ____________	20. ____________

Create a Word Search using these words. Share it with a friend.

Vocabulary Development 5

Name: ____________________

Date: ____________________

Media: ____________________

☐ Newspaper ☐ Magazine ☐ Internet Article ▶ TV Show ▶ Movie ▶ Video

Lights! Camera! Action!

The TV and filmmaking industry uses its own expressions in everyday work. Use the words in the Word Box to solve the puzzle.

pan	**dolly**	**tilt**	**framing**
set	**cutaways**	**props**	**freeze frame**
zoom	**wide angle**	**inserts**	

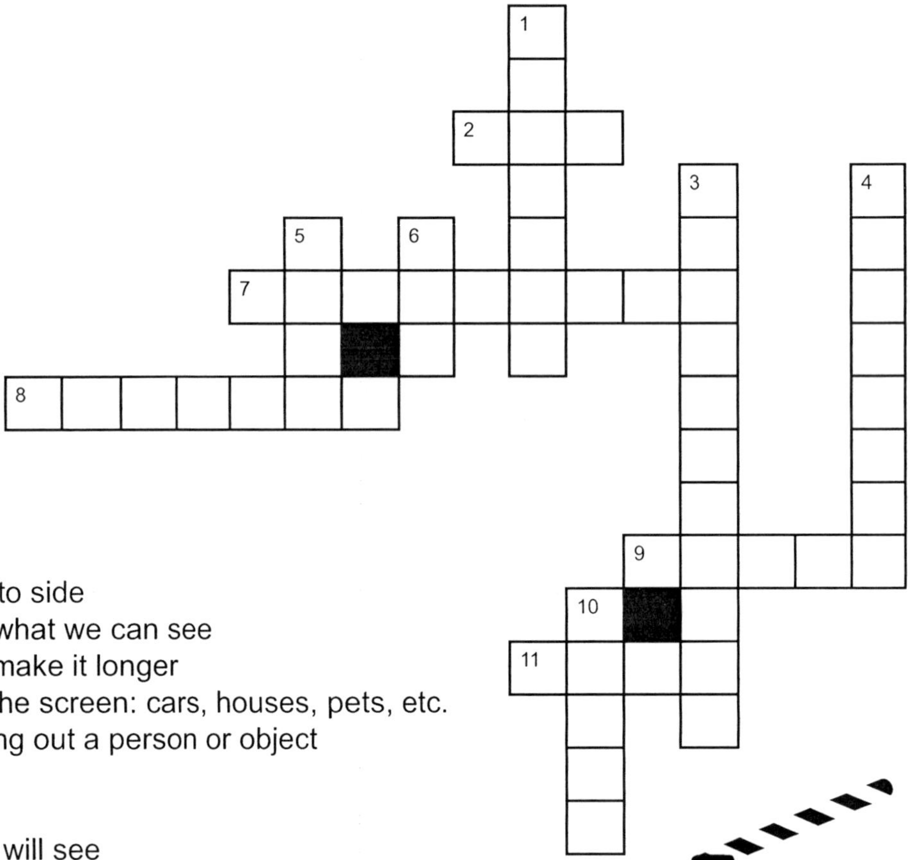

Across:

2. camera moving from side to side
7. moving out and widening what we can see
8. adding parts to a story to make it longer
9. all the objects we see on the screen: cars, houses, pets, etc.
11. moving in close and singling out a person or object

Down:

1. deciding what the camera will see
3. a moving picture becomes still and stays on the screen
4. taking out part of a scene to shorten the length of a story
5. camera moves up and down from top to bottom of an object
6. the location of a story or scene
10. camera (on wheels) moves away from, or with the action

Vocabulary Development 6

Name: ______________________
Date: ______________________
Media: ______________________

☐ Newspaper ☐ Magazine ☐ Internet Article
▶ TV Show ▶ Movie ▶ Video

All About Atmosphere

Producers of TV shows or movies try to create "atmosphere" or a mood to draw us into the story. They want us to feel a certain way and become a part of the story. They may do this through the characters, the dialogue, the lighting, the setting, and the sound effects. Some examples of mood are: suspense, fear, happiness, excitement, and mystery.

Pick a show to watch. Pay close attention to the atmosphere. Decide how the producer creates that atmosphere. Complete the chart by writing descriptions of these features that tell how the atmosphere was created.

Name of show: ____

Atmosphere: ____

Features	**Words and phrases to describe these features**
Characters	
Dialogue	
Lighting	
Setting	
Sound effects	

Vocabulary Development 7

Name: ______________________

Date: ______________________

Media: ______________________

▶ Newspaper ▶ TV Show
▶ Magazine ▶ Movie
▶ Internet Article ▶ Video

A Picture Is Worth 1000 Words

Select a picture from your media that you think gives the best idea of the story.

Find or think about adjectives that describe that picture. For example, adjectives can tell us size, shape, color, texture, age, physical features, and personality traits.

Write 25 adjectives that relate to your picture.

1. ______________________ 14. ______________________
2. ______________________ 15. ______________________
3. ______________________ 16. ______________________
4. ______________________ 17. ______________________
5. ______________________ 18. ______________________
6. ______________________ 19. ______________________
7. ______________________ 20. ______________________
8. ______________________ 21. ______________________
9. ______________________ 22. ______________________
10. ______________________ 23. ______________________
11. ______________________ 24. ______________________
12. ______________________ 25. ______________________
13. ______________________ **WOW!**

Vocabulary Development 8

Name: ____________________

Date: ____________________

Media: ____________________

- [x] Newspaper
- [x] Magazine
- [x] Internet Article
- [ ] TV Show
- [ ] Movie
- [ ] Video

Calling All Parts of Speech!

Read your article. Find words in your article that fit the categories on the chart.

Write your answers under the correct heading on the chart.

Name of article: ____

Proper Nouns	Common Nouns	Pronouns	Adjectives	Verbs	Adverbs

Vocabulary Development 9

Name: ______________________________

Date: ______________________________

Media: ______________________________

☐ Newspaper ▶ TV Show

☐ Magazine ▶ Movie

☐ Internet Article ▶ Video

Media Symbols

Before a program starts, we see symbols that give us information. Throughout the program, there will be breaks or messages for us.

In your own words, **define** these terms that are **symbols** or **breaks**. Give one specific example of each term from something you've seen.

Term	Meaning of the Term	An Example of the Term
Breaking news		
Commercial		
News, weather, or sports trailer		
Station break		
Station identification		
Viewer advisory		

Vocabulary Development 10

Name: ______________________________

Date: ______________________________

Media: ______________________________

- ☐ Newspaper
- ☐ Magazine
- ☐ Internet Article
- ▶ TV Show
- ▶ Movie
- ▶ Video

What's My Line?

Producing a TV show, movie, or video requires the skill of many people.

Before you view, read the list of occupations on the chart.
While you view, think about the job each person on the list might do.
After you view, give a definition or job description for each occupation listed.

Use a **dictionary** or the **Internet** to help you with your answers.

Occupation	Job Description
Camera man	
Casting agent	
Choreographer	
Director	
Stagehand	
Producer	
Prompter	
Scriptwriter	
Set designer	
Sound effects coordinator	

Vocabulary Development 11

Name: ______________________

Date: ______________________

Media: ______________________

☐ Newspaper ☒ TV Show
☐ Magazine ☐ Movie
☐ Internet Article ☐ Video

TV Types

There are many types of TV shows to entertain us.

Give a **definition** for each type of show listed on the chart.
Use a dictionary or the Internet to help you with your answers.

Then write one example of each type of show.

Type of TV show	Definition	Example
Cartoon		
Documentary		
Game show		
Infomercial		
Mini-series		
Music		
News		
Serial		
Sitcom		
Soap opera		
Sports		
Talk show		

Vocabulary Development 12

Name: ______________________

Date: ______________________

Media: ______________________

☐ Newspaper ☒ TV Show
☐ Magazine ☐ Movie
☐ Internet Article ☐ Video

Elements of a TV Show

There are different types of TV shows. A talk show has one or more hosts who talk about many topics and interview people. Talk shows usually have a live audience. Sitcom means "situational comedy" and is often about ordinary people living ordinary lives. Sitcoms may or may not be filmed before a live audience.

Pick an example of each type of show. Then complete the charts by defining each element of the show using an example you've seen.

Title of Talk Show:

Element	Meaning of Element
Celebrity guest	
Commercial break	
Host	
Live broadcast	
Studio audience	

Title of Sitcom:

Element	Meaning of Element
Laugh track	
Plot problem	
Regular cast	
Standard set	
Wrap up	

Identifying Important Information 1

Name: ______________________

Date: ______________________

Media: ______________________

- ▶ Newspaper
- ▶ Magazine
- ▶ Internet Article
- ☐ TV Show
- ☐ Movie
- ☐ Video

Article Reporting

Read your written media. Find the important facts in the article and complete the chart.

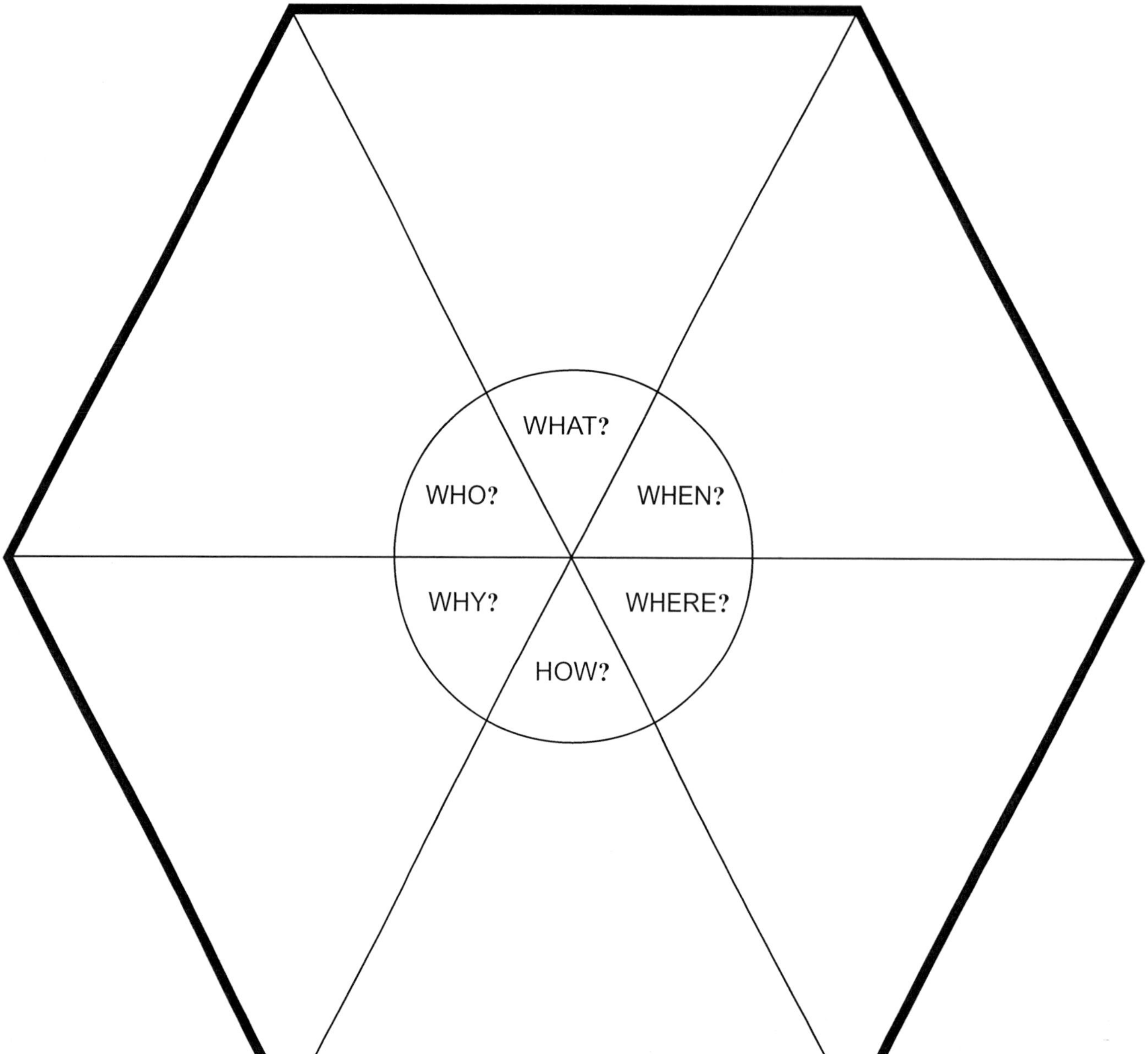

Identifying Important Information 2

Name: ____________________

Date: ____________________

Media: ____________________

- ▶ Newspaper
- ▶ Magazine
- ▶ Internet Article
- ☐ TV Show
- ☐ Movie
- ☐ Video

What's the Message?

Identify the main idea from the written text. Find four ideas that support the main message.

Main Idea

Supporting Idea

Supporting Idea

Supporting Idea

Supporting Idea

Identifying Important Information 3

Name: ______________________

Date: ______________________

Media: ______________________

☐ Newspaper ▶ TV Show

☐ Magazine ▶ Movie

☐ Internet Article ▶ Video

Analyzing the Message

Literary devices are used in written pieces but also in daily speech. They include verbal expressions, slang, idioms, metaphors, and similes. While you are watching a TV commercial, fill in this graphic organizer. Find the literary device(s) used. Write them below. Can you explain the literary device using everyday English language?

What Was Said?	Literary Device	What It Means in Everyday English

Identifying Important Information 4

Name: ______________________________

Date: ______________________________

Media: ______________________________

- [ ] Newspaper
- [ ] Magazine
- [ ] Internet Article
- [x] TV Show
- [ ] Movie
- [ ] Video

Who Is Your Target Audience?

While you are watching a TV commercial, fill in this graphic organizer. Can you tell who the intended targeted audience is?

Main character(s)	
Product	
Background music	
Language	
Narrator	
Mood of commercial	
Writing (choice of words)	
Tempo/beat	
Length of ad	
Time of appearance	
Channel/media	

Target audience is:

What details led you to this conclusion?

Identifying Important Information 5

Name: ______________________

Date: ______________________

Media: ______________________

- ▶ Newspaper
- ▶ Magazine
- ▶ Internet Article
- ☐ TV Show
- ☐ Movie
- ☐ Video

Problem Solver

Identify the problem in your article and the steps involved in finding the solution.

Problem:

Step 1

Step 2

Step 3

Solution:

Name: ______________________________
Date: ______________________________
Media: ______________________________

- ▶ Newspaper
- ▶ Magazine
- ▶ Internet Article
- ☐ TV Show
- ☐ Movie
- ☐ Video

Behind the Scenes

Look at an ad in a magazine or on the Internet. Break down the ad into the process the publishing company might have taken into consideration when they created the ad. Ask yourself questions such as: Is the font important in the ad? Are people in the ad? Is the ad believable? Is the slogan catchy? Is the colour scheme appropriate? Is there too much fine print?

1.

2.

3.

4.

5.

6.

What important characteristics did the publishing company use?

____
____
____
____
____
____
____
____
____
____

If you could change the ad, what changes would you make?

____
____
____
____
____
____
____
____
____
____

Identifying Important Information 7

Name: ______________________

Date: ______________________

Media: ______________________

▶ Newspaper	☐ TV Show
▶ Magazine	☐ Movie
▶ Internet Article	☐ Video

Picture Analysis

Paste a picture in the box below. Write five conclusions you come up with by looking at the picture. Would you trust the product? Are the people credible? What type of person do you think this person is? What secrets are they trying to hide?

1.
2.
3.
4.
5.

Hide your conclusions and have a classmate come up with five conclusions of their own. Compare your conclusions. Were they similar? Different?

Identifying Important Information 8

Name: ______________________________

Date: ______________________________

Media: ______________________________

▶ Newspaper ☐ TV Show

▶ Magazine ☐ Movie

▶ Internet Article ☐ Video

Changing Consumers

Find an ad from a newspaper, magazine, or the Internet. Using the same picture(s), **rewrite** the ad for another type of customer.

Original Ad (Summary):

____

New Version of the Ad:

____

Identifying Important Information 9

Name: ______________________________

Date: ______________________________

Media: ______________________________

- ▶ Newspaper
- ▶ Magazine
- ▶ Internet Article
- ☐ TV Show
- ☐ Movie
- ☐ Video

Five Senses

Some ads have a way of awaking your senses. Choose an ad that you like. What senses do you feel when you view the ad? Write your feelings in the appropriate box.

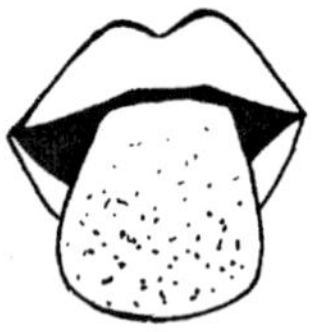

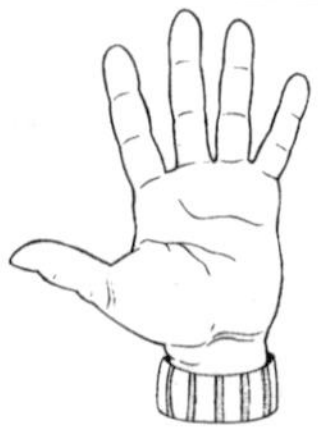

Identifying Important Information 10

Name: ______________________

Date: ______________________

Media: ______________________

- ▶ Newspaper
- ▶ Magazine
- ▶ Internet Article
- ☐ TV Show
- ☐ Movie
- ☐ Video

Cause and Effect Fishbone

Choose the most important event that happened in your article. Write the event on the backbone of the fish. Now, on the scales, write the things that caused this event to happen.

Character Analysis 1

Name: ____________________

Date: ____________________

Media: ____________________

☐ Newspaper ▶ TV Show
☐ Magazine ▶ Movie
☐ Internet Article ▶ Video

Personality Web

List six character traits of the main character from a TV show or movie. What is he or she like? How does he or she act? How does he or she feel? What trait do you especially like? Which trait do you dislike?

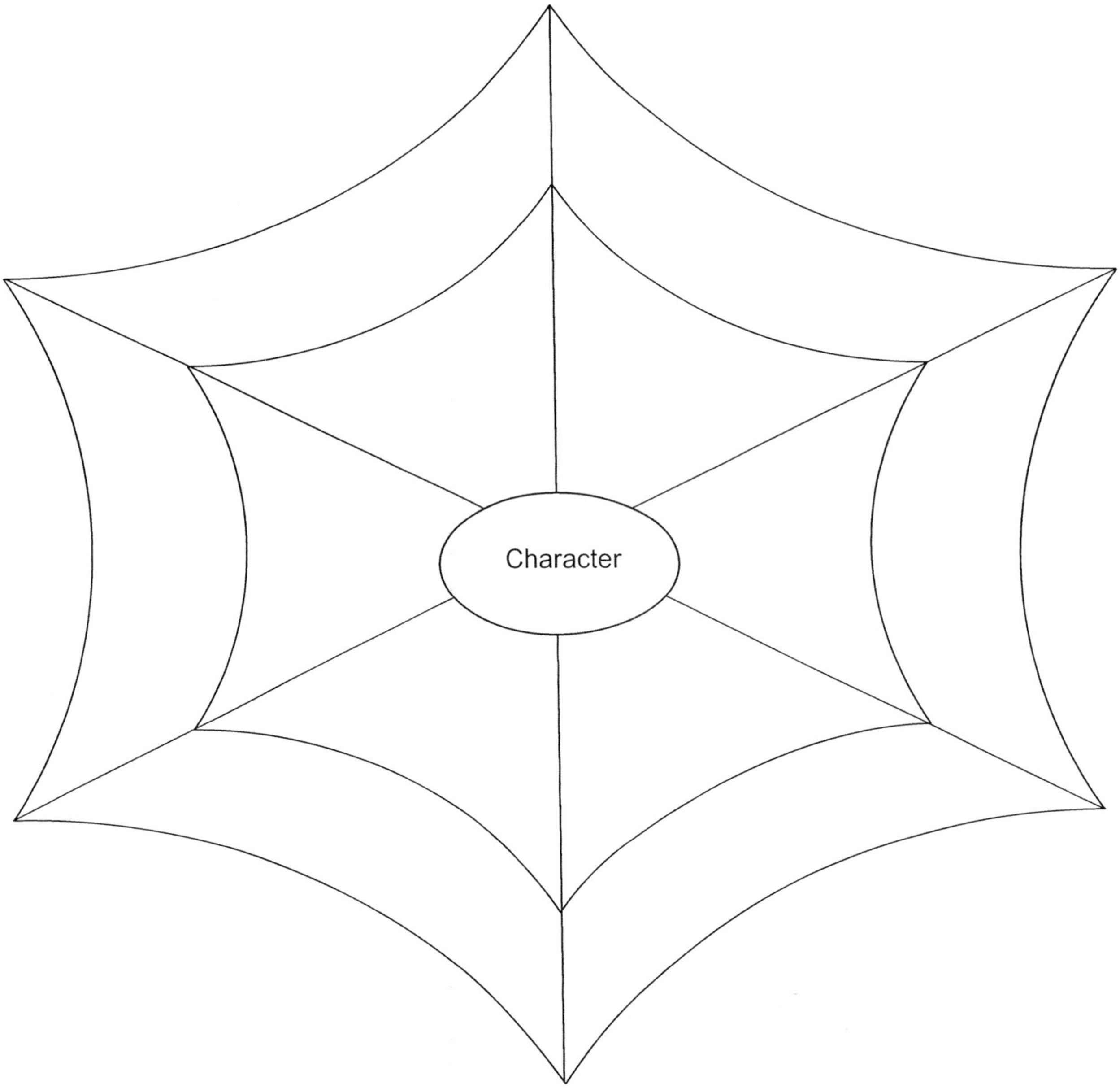

Character Analysis 2

Name: ______________________________

Date: ______________________________

Media: ______________________________

- ☐ Newspaper
- ☐ Magazine
- ☐ Internet Article
- ▶ TV Show
- ▶ Movie
- ▶ Video

Character's Behavior Evidence

Sometimes people says things and they actually mean the opposite. Watch a TV show or a movie. Using a quote from one of the characters, write two possible meanings of what the character said.

Quote:

Actual meaning of the quote:

Underlying message in the quote:

What would you have said to express the same meaning?

Character Analysis 3

Name: ______________________

Date: ______________________

Media: ______________________

☐ Newspaper ☐ Magazine ☐ Internet Article ▶ TV Show ▶ Movie ▶ Video

Addition of a New Character

Choose a TV show, film, or movie and add a new character. Fill in the background information below. Write how and where this character will fit in with the existing characters.

Name:	Gender:	Age:
	Height:	Weight:
Hair Color:	Eye Color:	
Physical Details:		
Character Trait:	Character Trait:	
Character Trait:	Character Trait:	
Character Trait:	Character Trait:	
Connections to Other Characters:		

Character Analysis 4

Name: ____________________________

Date: ____________________________

Media: ____________________________

▶ Newspaper ▶ TV Show

▶ Magazine ▶ Movie

▶ Internet Article ▶ Video

People Behind the Scenes

There are many different types of jobs in media where the workers are hidden behind the scenes. Choose a media occupation. **Write five interview questions** to collect more information on that person's job. Find a person that currently holds that job and e-mail them your questions.

1.

2.

3.

4.

5.

Interview questions sent to : ____________________________

E-mail subject: ____________________________ Date: ______________

Response received on: ____________________________

Analyze the answers you received. Did anything surprise you? Did you learn anything new? Would this type of job interest you?

Character Analysis 5

Name: ______________________________

Date: ______________________________

Media: ______________________________

- Newspaper
- Magazine
- Internet Article
- TV Show
- Movie
- Video

Character Comparison

Choose a character that you have both read about and watched. List the unique characteristics of each character and their similarities.

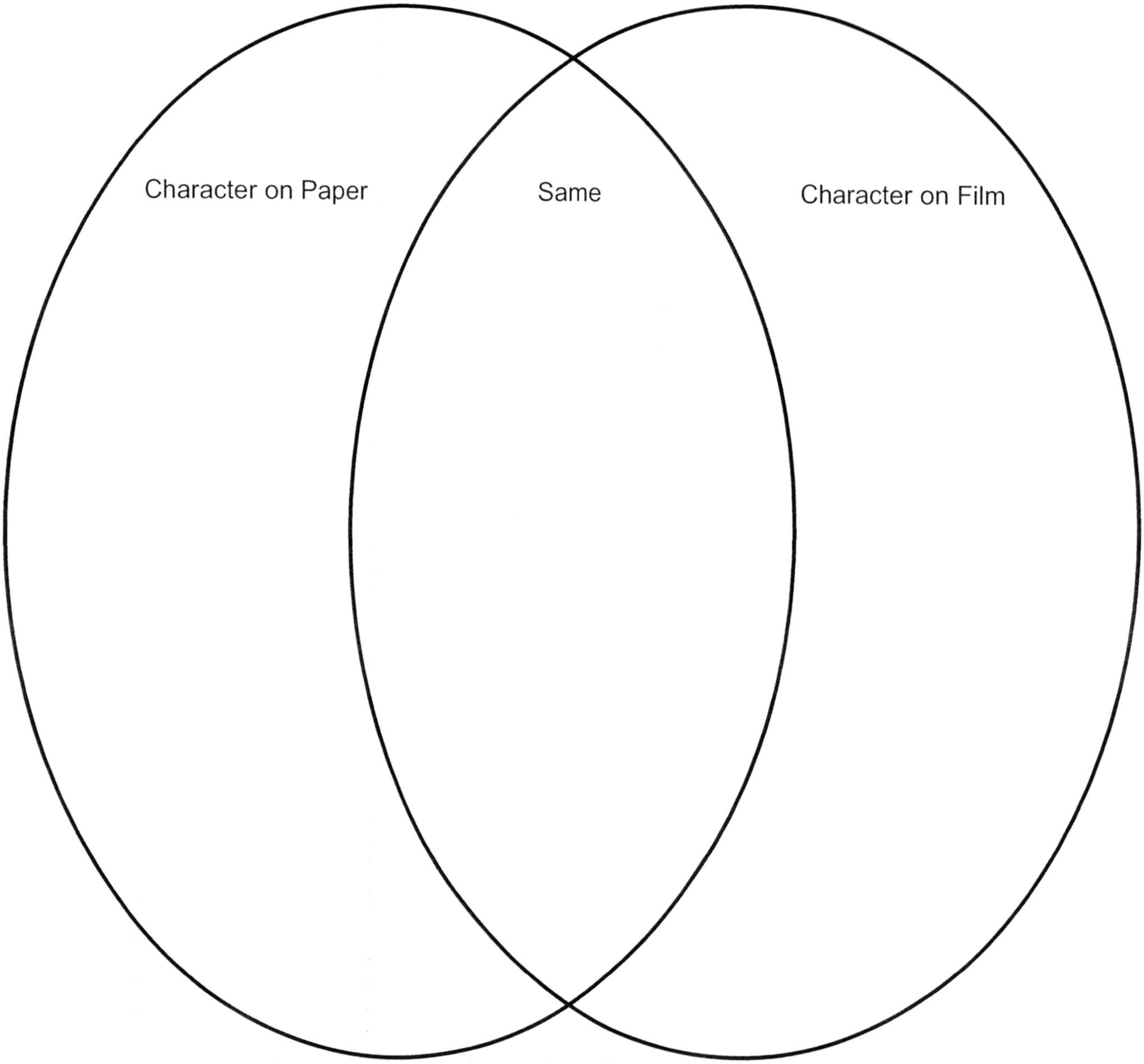

Character Analysis 6

Name: ______________________

Date: ______________________

Media: ______________________

- ▶ Newspaper
- ▶ Magazine
- ▶ Internet Article
- ☐ TV Show
- ☐ Movie
- ☐ Video

Nonfiction into Fiction

Choose an ad or article from a newspaper, magazine, or the Internet. Use the character as the main character within **a fictional story**. What genre of story will you write? Remember your story should include a beginning, a middle, and an end.

Character Analysis 7

Name: ______________________

Date: ______________________

Media: ______________________

☐ Newspaper ☐ Magazine ☐ Internet Article

▶ TV Show ▶ Movie ▶ Video

True or False

Create a list of five statements about a character from a TV show, movie, or news bulletin. Ask a partner to decide if the statements are true or false.

TRUE	FALSE	1.
TRUE	FALSE	2.
TRUE	FALSE	3.
TRUE	FALSE	4.
TRUE	FALSE	5.

Give supporting evidence to prove that the statements you have chosen above are True or False.

Proof
1.
2.
3.
4.
5.

Character Analysis 8

Name: ____________________

Date: ____________________

Media: ____________________

- ▶ Newspaper
- ▶ Magazine
- ▶ Internet Article
- ▶ TV Show
- ▶ Movie
- ▶ Video

My Friend

Choose a character from a magazine article, an ad, a TV commercial, or a TV show/movie. Write below the qualities you like and dislike about this character.

LIKES	DISLIKES

Analyze if this character could be your friend. Do you have much in common? Do you share any qualities? Why would you be friends, or not, with this character?

Character Analysis 9

Name: ____________________

Date: ____________________

Media: ____________________

- Newspaper
- Magazine
- Internet Article
- TV Show
- Movie
- Video

Write a Letter of Advice

After reading about someone in a magazine or seeing them on TV, write a letter and offer some form of advice.

Person's Name: ____________________ Seen in: ____________________

Dear ____________________ ,

Character Analysis 10

Name: ______________________

Date: ______________________

Media: ______________________

- Newspaper
- Magazine
- Internet Article
- TV Show
- Movie
- Video

What Would YOU Do?

Write a paragraph about what a character has done or said that impressed you.

Now write about yourself replacing that character. What changes would there be? What similar reactions would you have? What differences would there be?

Character Analysis 11

Name: ______________________

Date: ______________________

Media: ______________________

- ▶ Newspaper
- ▶ TV Show
- ▶ Magazine
- ▶ Movie
- ▶ Internet Article
- ▶ Video

The Ins and Outs of the Character

Watch a TV show/movie that you are not familiar with for the duration of time between two sets of commercials. Describe what you learned about the character from briefly watching the show.

Watch the entire TV show.

Now describe the character's behavior. Was your first impression accurate? Did the character continue to behave in the same fashion? Or was the later behavior different? If so, how?

Character Analysis 12

Name: ____________________

Date: ____________________

Media: ____________________

▶ Newspaper ▶ TV Show

▶ Magazine ▶ Movie

▶ Internet Article ▶ Video

Biography

Write a biography based on a famous actor or character you have seen in an ad, a movie, or a TV show. Use a timeline to help you organize the important dates.

TIMELINE: Space out and write numbers in periods of 5 years.

__________ / __________ / __________ / __________ / __________

BIOGRAPHY of: ____________________

Summarizing Events 1

Name: ____________________________

Date: ____________________________

Media: ____________________________

▶ Newspaper ▶ TV Show
▶ Magazine ▶ Movie
▶ Internet Article ▶ Video

Story Trail

Think about the events in your story or article. Make a "trail" of events by writing one main event in each of the boxes.

1.

2.

3.

4.

Title: ______________________________

5.

6.

Summarizing Events 2

Name: ______________________
Date: ______________________
Media: ______________________

▶ Newspaper ▶ TV Show
▶ Magazine ▶ Movie
▶ Internet Article ▶ Video

It Goes Like This!

Think about the events in your story or article. Write a summary of the most important events or facts. Use these connective words.

First, ____

____

Then,____

____

Next,____

____

After that, ____

____

And then, ____

____

Finally, ____

____

What was the most important event or idea in this story? Give a reason for your choice.

____

____

____

____

____

____

Summarizing Events 3

Name: ______________________

Date: ______________________

Media: ______________________

▶ Newspaper ▶ Magazine ▶ Internet Article ▶ TV Show ▶ Movie ▶ Video

It's All About Time!

Write a summary based on events in a movie, a TV show, or an article. Use a timeline to help you organize the important dates.

Date/time	Event

Now write a summary of events. Include the dates or times in your summary.

____

____

____

____

____

____

____

____

Name: ______________________________

Date: ______________________________

Media: ______________________________

- Newspaper
- Magazine
- Internet Article
- TV Show
- Movie
- Video

Comic Strip

Retell your article or program in a comic strip. Use pictures and add dialogue.

Title : ____

1.	2.	3.
4.	5.	6.
7.	8.	9.

Summarizing Events 5

Name: ______________________

Date: ______________________

Media: ______________________

▶ Newspaper ▶ TV Show
▶ Magazine ▶ Movie
▶ Internet Article ▶ Video

Bookmark Organizer

Make a bookmark using a heavy paper or light cardboard. On the back of the bookmark, write the **title** of your show or article and the type of **media**. Tell about each of the **main events** in the order they happened. On the front of the bookmark, illustrate your sentences.

back

TITLE of SHOW or ARTICLE

Media

Main Events

1. ______________________
____
____

2. ______________________
____
____

3. ______________________
____
____

4. ______________________
____
____

5. ______________________
____
____

front

Summarizing Events 6

Name: ______________________

Date: ______________________

Media: ______________________

☐ Newspaper ☒ TV Show

☐ Magazine ☒ Movie

☐ Internet Article ☒ Video

Nonfiction Report

Watch your favorite show on a learning channel or watch a movie about true facts. Complete the chart to summarize the facts in the order they appeared in the show.

Title of show: ______________________

Type of content: (science, history) ______________________

Main topic: ______________________

	Facts
1.	
2.	
3.	
4.	
5.	
6.	
7.	
8.	

Think of a question you still have about this topic. Write your question here.

____

____

____

____

Summarizing Events 7

Name: ______________________

Date: ______________________

Media: ______________________

- ▶ Newspaper
- ▶ Magazine
- ▶ Internet Article
- ☐ TV Show
- ☐ Movie
- ☐ Video

Extra! Extra!

A good newspaper reporter always includes the 5 W's and How? in a report.

Pretend you are a reporter writing an article for the school newspaper or for the news bulletin board.

After reading an article or watching a show, complete the chart with the basic facts. Then use these facts to write your news report.

Who?	What?	Where?

When?	Why?	How?

My report title: ____

____

____

____

____

Summarizing Events 8

Name: ______________________

Date: ______________________

Media: ______________________

▶ Newspaper ☐ TV Show

▶ Magazine ☐ Movie

▶ Internet Article ☐ Video

Sentence Sum Up

A **topic sentence** grabs our interest and tells us what the paragraph is going to be about. It is the first sentence of the paragraph.

1. **Read** your article. **Highlight** the **first sentence** of each paragraph.

2. **Reread** just the **highlighted topic sentences**. Do they make a **good summary**?
   If so, write those sentences, in paragraph form, on the lines below.
   If not, rewrite those sentences, in paragraph form, on the lines below.

Title: ____

Why do you think it is so important to have good topic sentences?

Summarizing Events 9

Name: ______________________

Date: ______________________

Media: ______________________

- ▶ Newspaper
- ▶ Magazine
- ▶ Internet Article
- ☐ TV Show
- ☐ Movie
- ☐ Video

The Funnies!

Pick a comic strip to **read**. **Cut ou**t the pictures, removing the dialogue as you cut. **Paste** the pictures in the boxes below in any order. **Write new dialogue** for the characters to tell your own story.

Title: ____

Name: ______________________
Date: ______________________
Media: ______________________

- [x] Newspaper
- [x] Magazine
- [x] Internet Article
- [ ] TV Show
- [ ] Movie
- [ ] Video

Find and Flag!

Read your article. **Circle, underline,** or **highlight** at least five **key words** in each paragraph of your article.

Write a summary of your article by using these key words. Use connecting words and complete sentences.

Key words:

Summary:

____
____
____
____
____
____
____
____
____
____
____
____
____
____
____
____

Reasoning and Critical Thinking 1

Name: ______________________

Date: ______________________

Media: ______________________

☐ Newspaper ▶ TV Show

☐ Magazine ▶ Movie

☐ Internet Article ▶ Video

My TV Show

The more TV sitcoms you watch the more you can create and develop your own sitcom. **Develop** an outline for a new TV sitcom. Describe the setting, the characters, and the plot. Explain why you believe this sitcom will become a hit TV show. Use the word box below if you need.

setting	**characters**	**theme**	**style**
house, trailer, car, apartment, school, campground, park, garage, bedroom	boy, girl, sister, brother, parents, extended family, friends, teachers, workers, community workers	kids in school kids on a sports team kids at home kids in a band	drama funny trauma musical

Setting:

Main Character:

Minor Character:

Minor Character:

Plot:

Style:

Name: ____________________

Date: ____________________

Media: ____________________

- [ ] Newspaper
- [ ] Magazine
- [ ] Internet Article
- [x] TV Show
- [ ] Movie
- [ ] Video

For Your Information

Before you do this activity you will need some information from the television program guide.

Pick a show you like. Read and copy the information from the guide.

Title of show: ____________________

Information from Guide: ____________________

____

Using this information as a clue, predict what you think will happen in the show.
Write your predictions below.

____

____

____

____

Now watch your show. Which of your predictions were right?

____

____

____

____

Which of your predictions were incorrect?

____

____

____

____

Reasoning and Critical Thinking 3

Name: ______________________

Date: ______________________

Media: ______________________

☐ Newspaper ☐ Magazine ☐ Internet Article ▶ TV Show ▶ Movie ▶ Video

What to Watch

Pretend you are working for a newspaper and your job is to write a column about movies. You want to suggest good movies to watch. You want to give people some information without giving away the story.

Fill in the necessary information in the header. Write a description of a good movie you would recommend. Include a summary of the story and a description of the characters, setting, and plot. Tell why you would recommend it.

What to Watch in Movie Land

By: ______________________

Title: ______________________

Stars: ______________________

Name: ______________________________

Date: ______________________________

Media: ______________________________

☐ Newspaper ☒ TV Show

☐ Magazine ☐ Movie

☐ Internet Article ☐ Video

Dear Producer

Write a letter to the producer of your favorite TV show.
Tell him/her that you have some ideas for what should happen in the upcoming shows.
Outline your ideas in the letter.

Dear Producer of ____

____

____

____

____

____

____

____

____

____

____

____

____

____

____

____

____

____

Your fan, ______________________________

Name: ____________________

Date: ____________________

Media: ____________________

- Newspaper
- TV Show
- Magazine
- Movie
- Internet Article
- Video

Fact or Opinion

Create a list of six statements about information from a documentary TV show, movie, news bulletin, or article.

Decide if the statements are fact or opinion, and explain your reasoning.
Complete the chart.

Title: ____

Statement	Fact	Opinion	My reasoning
1.			
2.			
3.			
4.			
5.			
6.			

Reasoning and Critical Thinking 6

Name: ______________________

Date: ______________________

Media: ______________________

▶ Newspaper ☐ TV Show

▶ Magazine ☐ Movie

▶ Internet Article ☐ Video

KWLQ

Read the title of your article. Complete the first two columns: **what you know** about the subject and **what you would like to know**. Read the article. Now complete the last two columns of the chart. **What did you learn**? What **questions do you still have**?

Title of article: ____

Main topic of this article: ____

Know	**W**ant to Know	**L**earned	**Q**uestions I Still Have

Reasoning and Critical Thinking 7

Name: ______________________

Date: ______________________

Media: ______________________

- ☐ Newspaper
- ☐ Magazine
- ☒ Internet Article
- ☐ TV Show
- ☐ Movie
- ☐ Video

Believe It or Not!

The Internet is a great learning tool. We can research topics, read articles for fun, and even share information. Sometimes younger students have a hard time knowing what information that they read should be believed.

Write a **What to Believe Guide** for young readers. Make a list of **Do's** and **Don'ts** about what we read on the Internet.

Dear Young Reader,

I want to help you with your reading of Internet information. Here are my tips:

Do:

____

Don't:

____

Reasoning and Critical Thinking 8

Name: ______________________

Date: ______________________

Media: ______________________

▶ Newspaper ▶ TV Show

▶ Magazine ▶ Movie

▶ Internet Article ▶ Video

Ad Awareness

Find and cut out an ad for a movie you will watch. Paste the ad in the box below. Make a prediction about the movie in the ad. Fill in the boxes below.

Movie ad

Predict how much you will enjoy this movie.

What do you believe will happen in the movie?

How do you think you will react to this movie?

Once you have seen the movie, tell how close your initial prediction was. Was the ad a good representation of the movie? Why or why not? What changes would you make to the ad?

Reasoning and Critical Thinking 9

Name: ______________________

Date: ______________________

Media: ______________________

☐ Newspaper ☑ TV Show
☐ Magazine ☐ Movie
☐ Internet Article ☐ Video

Adding Important Details

Reporters cover the NEWS in terms of “stories” that have a beginning, middle, and end. Each story also has main characters, minor characters, a setting, and a plot. Journalists have the duty to report the news and some add details to make the story more interesting. Watch a few segments of your local news. Choose one segment. Fill in the boxes below with the details about the story. Add what you would to make your story more spectacular and clearer.

Details in the News Clip	Details I Would Add

Name: ______________________________

Date: ______________________________

Media: ______________________________

- ▶ Newspaper
- ▶ Magazine
- ▶ Internet Article
- ☐ TV Show
- ☐ Movie
- ☐ Video

Emotions

When watching movies, we feel at least four or five different emotions Write a summary of your favorite movie or a sequel using as many of the emotion words provided as you can.

EMOTIONS
(Intense to Mild)

loved, adored, idolized, alive, wanted, lustful, worthy, pity, respected, empathy, awed, enthusiastic, zealous, courageous, enchanted, ardor, infatuated, tender, vibrant, independent, capable, happy, proud, gratified, worthy, sympathetic, important, concerned, appreciated, consoled, delighted, eager, optimistic, joyful, courage, hopeful, valiant, brave, brilliant, liked, cared for, esteemed, affectionate, fond, excited, patient, strong, gay, inspired, anticipating, amused, yearning, popular, peaceful, appealing, determined, pleased, excited, jolly, relieved, glad, adventurous, peaceful, intelligent, friendly, regarded, benevolent, wide awake, at ease, relaxed, comfortable, content, keen, amazed, alert, sure, attractive, approved, untroubled, graceful, turned on, warm, amused, daring, comfortable, smart, interested

____
____
____
____
____
____
____
____
____
____
____
____
____
____
____
____
____
____
____
____
____
____

Creativity and Design 1

Name: ______________________

Date: ______________________

Media: ______________________

▶ Newspaper ▶ TV Show

▶ Magazine ▶ Movie

▶ Internet Article ▶ Video

Putting the Best Foot Forward

Look at the publicity flyers you receive at home along with your mail. You have been hired to create a tri-fold paper publicity flyer for the up upcoming elections. Decide who is running, level of government, and qualities this person may have. Include other important information to inform the public and put this person's best assets forward. Create the rough draft in the boxes below.

2.	3.	4.
5.	last page/credits 6.	cover page 1.

Creativity and Design 2

Name: ____________________

Date: ____________________

Media: ____________________

▶ Newspaper ▶ TV Show

▶ Magazine ▶ Movie

▶ Internet Article ▶ Video

Design a Costume

Draw or sketch a character from a commercial or TV show wearing a newly created costume. Explain why the character should wear this new costume or outfit.

Creativity and Design 3

Name: ______________________________

Date: ______________________________

Media: ______________________________

☐ Newspaper ☐ Magazine ☐ Internet Article

▶ TV Show ▶ Movie ▶ Video

Photo Journal

Using colorful pictures from magazines or the Internet, illustrate and create a story line to be used for a new TV show or commercial. Use the boxes below to help you set up your images by sketching out your ideas with stick drawings or keywords. You will need to work on additional plain white papers for your finished pieces.

1.	2.	3.	4.

1. ______________________________
2. ______________________________
3. ______________________________
4. ______________________________

5.	6.	7.	8.

5. ______________________________
6. ______________________________
7. ______________________________
8. ______________________________

Creativity and Design 4

Name: ____________________

Date: ____________________

Media: ____________________

☐ Newspaper ▶ TV Show

☐ Magazine ▶ Movie

☐ Internet Article ▶ Video

Create a TV Schedule

Look at your local TV listings in the weekly booklet or in the entertainment section of your local paper. You have just been hired as the TV programmer of your favorite TV channel. You must now schedule the prime time shows for the week. Your schedule must contain a variety of shows. You cannot have the same show back-to-back. Each day has to be different but the news must be on every day at the same time. Use real TV shows. Compare your schedule with a friend. How similar or different are they?

	MONDAY	TUESDAY	WEDNESDAY	THURSDAY	FRIDAY
6:00					
7:00					
8:00					
9:00					
10:00					

Creativity and Design 5

Name: ____________________

Date: ____________________

Media: ____________________

- ☐ Newspaper
- ☐ Magazine
- ☐ Internet Article
- ☒ TV Show
- ☐ Movie
- ☐ Video

And the Survey Says…

There are many quiz-like game shows on TV today. After you have identified a few game/quiz shows and their question format, complete the following activity. You have been hired by an advertising firm to find out what is in or out with today's kids. The company wants to know what kids in your school at your grade level like and dislike. You will now create a survey asking fellow classmates what they like, dislike, buy, would like to buy, and already own. Once your consumer habit questions are written, ask five students in your class the questions. Prepare a summary of the wants, needs, likes, and dislikes.

1.
2.
3.
4.
5.
6.
7.
8.
9.
10.

Survey Summary Report:

Creativity and Design 6

Name: ______________________

Date: ______________________

Media: ______________________

- ☑ Newspaper
- ☑ Magazine
- ☑ Internet Article
- ☐ TV Show
- ☐ Movie
- ☐ Video

Switching the Feelings

Choose an article or an ad that has caught your eye. Rewrite the article below by changing the emotions felt in the article. If the article was funny – make it sad. If the article was sad – make it angry. Rewrite the article to evoke another feeling other than what the author originally intended.

Creativity and Design 7

Name: ______________________

Date: ______________________

Media: ______________________

☐ Newspaper
☐ Magazine
☐ Internet Article
▶ TV Show
▶ Movie
▶ Video

Movie Poster

Choose a movie that you really don't like. Create a movie poster for this movie to help increase viewing and revenues. How will you portray this movie in a positive light?

Name: ______________________
Date: ______________________
Media: ______________________

- [ ] Newspaper
- [x] Magazine
- [ ] Internet Article
- [x] TV Show
- [x] Movie
- [ ] Video

Create a Slogan

Brainstorm a few product slogans that have caught your eye either on TV, in movies, or in magazines. Create a new product. Along with this new product, you will need a new catchy slogan and a written advertisement.

New Product

Catchy slogan:

____
____
____
____
____
____
____
____
____
____
____

Advertisement: ______________________

____
____
____
____
____
____
____
____

Creativity and Design 9

Name: ______________________

Date: ______________________

Media: ______________________

- [ ] Newspaper
- [x] TV Show
- [ ] Magazine
- [ ] Movie
- [ ] Internet Article
- [ ] Video

Jingle Along

You have been hired to publicize a long time existing product. The company wants you to spruce up their image and create a new jingle to grab their customers' attention.

Product: ______________________

Cut and paste a picture of the product here.

Old Jingle:

New Jingle, written to this famous tune:

Name: ______________________
Date: ______________________
Media: ______________________

☐ Newspaper ☑ TV Show
☐ Magazine ☑ Movie
☐ Internet Article ☑ Video

Change the Ending

Choose a TV show, film, or movie that you have just watched. Write the story plot up until the problem. Now continue writing and give it a creative, different, and original ending.

Original Plot:

New Ending:

Creativity and Design 11

Name: ______________________

Date: ______________________

Media: ______________________

- Newspaper
- Magazine
- Internet Article
- TV Show
- Movie
- Video

Picture Book Design

Choose an article or a short movie that you have enjoyed. Create a picture book based on this story. Use the boxes below to help you set up your images by sketching out your ideas with stick drawings or keywords. You may need to work on additional plain white papers for your finished pieces. Rewrite the written piece to make the content more accessible to younger children. When you are done, read your picture book to a child in kindergarten, grade one, or grade two.

1. ______________________
2. ______________________
3. ______________________
4. ______________________

5. ______________________
6. ______________________
7. ______________________
8. ______________________